# SPANISH
## Phrasebook for Kids

T0371286

# About this book

Jane Wightwick
had the idea

Wina Gunn
wrote the pages

Leila & Zeinah Gaafar
(aged 10 and 12) drew
the first pictures in
each chapter

Robert Bowers
(aged 52) drew the other
pictures, and designed
the book

Ana Bremon
did the Spanish stuff

Important things
that must be included

© g-and-w publishing 2013

All rights reserved. This publication or any part of it may
not be copied or reproduced by any means without the
prior permission of the publisher. All enquiries should
be directed to the publisher.

A CIP catalogue record for this book is available from
the British Library

ISBN 978-0-7495-8369-9

Published by AA Publishing (a trading name of
AA Media Limited, whose registered office is
Grove House, Lutyens Close, Basingstoke, Hampshire
RG24 8AG. Registered number 06112600).

Printed and bound in China by
1010 Printing International Limited

A05864

my big brother mi hermano mayor
🗣 mee airmano my-yor

grandpa
abuelo
🗣 abwelo

grandma
abuela
🗣 abwela

dad
papá
🗣 pa-pah

mum mamá
🗣 ma-mah

my little sister
mi hermana pequeña
🗣 mee airmana
pekenya

MAKING FRIENDS

## Half a step this way

stepfather/stepmother
padrastro/madrastra
💋 padrastro/madrastra

stepbrother/stepsister
hermanastro/hermanastra
💋 airmanastro/airmanastra

half brother/half sister
medio hermano/medio hermana
💋 medyo airmano/
medyo airmana

Hi!
¡Hola!
💋 ola

What's your name?
¿Cómo te llamas?
💋 komo tay yamas

My name's ...
Me llamo ...
💋 may yamo

8

The Spanish put an upside-down question mark before a question, as well as one the right way up at the end. It's the same with exclamation marks.
¿Isn't that weird?   ¡You bet!

Are you OK?
¿Estás bien?
estas beeyen

Cool, and you?
Guay, ¿y tú?
gwhy. ee too

Where are you from?
¿De dónde eres?
day donday air-res

from Canada
de Canadá
 day canadah

from Ireland
de Irlanda
 day eerlanda

from Wales del País de Gales
 del pie-yis day gal-les
That means "the land of the Gauls".

from Scotland
de Escocia
 day escothya

from the United States
de los Estados Unidos
 day los estados ooneedos

from England
de Inglaterra
 day eengla-tairra

10

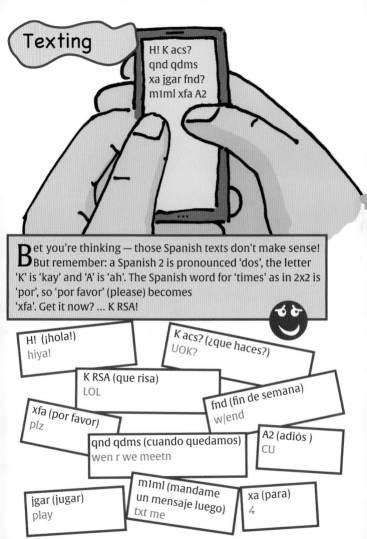

Texting

> H! K acs?
> qnd qdms
> xa jgar fnd?
> m1ml xfa A2

**B**et you're thinking — those Spanish texts don't make sense! But remember: a Spanish 2 is pronounced 'dos', the letter 'K' is 'kay' and 'A' is 'ah'. The Spanish word for 'times' as in 2x2 is 'por', so 'por favor' (please) becomes 'xfa'. Get it now? ... K RSA!

H! (¡hola!)
hiya!

K acs? (¿que haces?)
UOK?

K RSA (que risa)
LOL

fnd (fin de semana)
w/end

xfa (por favor)
plz

qnd qdms (cuando quedamos)
wen r we meetn

A2 (adiós )
CU

jgar (jugar)
play

m1ml (mandame un mensaje luego)
txt me

xa (para)
4

How old are you?
¿Cuántos años tienes?
🗣 kwantos anyos tee-enes

12 years old
Doce años
🗣 dothay anyos

Happy birthday!
¡Cumpleaños feliz!
🗣 koomplay-anyos faileeth

What's your star sign?
¿Qué signo del zodiaco eres?
🗣 kay signo del thodee-ako air-res

When's your birthday?
¿Cuándo es tu cumpleaños?
🗣 kwando es too koomplay-anyos

# Star signs

## AQUARIUS

Jan. 21 – Feb. 19
Acuario 💋 akwaree-o

## PISCES

Feb. 20 – Mar. 20
Piscis 💋 pees-thees

## ARIES

Mar. 21 – Apr. 20
Aries 💋 a-rees

## TAURUS

Apr. 21 – May. 21
Tauro 💋 towro

## GEMINI

May 22 – June 21
Géminis 💋 hemeenees

## CANCER

June 22 – July 23
Cáncer 💋 kanthair

## LEO

July 24 – Aug. 23
Leo 💋 leo

## VIRGO

Aug. 24 – Sep. 23
Virgo 💋 beergo

## LIBRA

Sep. 24 – Oct. 23
Libra 💋 leebra

## SCORPIO

Oct. 24 – Nov. 22
Escorpio 💋 eskorpee-o

## SAGITTARIUS

Nov. 23 – Dec. 21
Sagitario 💋 sa-heetaree-o

## CAPRICORN

Dec. 22 – Jan. 20
Capricornio 💋 kapreecornee-o

13

football el fútbol
🗣 el footbol

rollerblading
el patinaje en línea
🗣 el patee-nahay
en leenya

music
la música
🗣 la mooseeka

electronic games
los juegos electrónicos
🗣 los hway-gos elektroneekos

tv
la tele
🗣 la taylay

comics
los tebeos
🗣 los taybayos

school el colegio
🗣 el kolay-
heeyo

spiders las arañas
🗣 las aranyas

15

What's your ...?
¿Cuál es tu ...?
👄 kwal es too ...

favourite group
grupo preferido
👄 groopo prefereedo

favourite colour
color preferido
👄 kol-lor prefereedo

Page 69

favourite game
juego preferido
👄 hway-go prefereedo

**favourite food**
comida preferida
🗨 komeeda prefereeda

**favourite ringtone**
tono preferido
🗨 tone-oh prefereedo

animal

**favourite animal**
animal preferido
🗨 anee-mal prefereedo

**favourite team**
equipo preferido
🗨 ekeepo prefereedo

17

# Talk about your pets

**He's hungry**
Está hambriento
🗣 esta
ambree-yento

**Can I stroke your dog?**
¿Puedo acariciar tu perro?
🗣 pwedo atharee-thyar
too pair-ro

**She's sleeping**
Está durmiendo
🗣 esta doormee-yendo

**Do you have any pets?**
¿Tienes alguna mascota?
🗣 tee-enes
algoona mascota

cat
el gato
🗨️ el gato

dog
el perro
🗨️ el pair-ro

snake
la serpiente
🗨️ la serpee-entay

guinea pig
la cobaya
🗨️ la kob-eye-a

hamster
el hámster
🗨️ el hamstair

parakeet
el periquito
🗨️ el peree-keeto

## My little doggy goes guau guau!

A Spanish doggy (that's "guauguau" in baby language) doesn't say "woof, woof", it says *"guau, guau"* (*gwa-oo, gwa-oo*). A Spanish bird says *"pío, pío"* (*pee-o, pee-o*) and "cock-a-doodle-do" in Spanish chicken-speak is *"kikirikí"* (*kee-kee ree-kee*). But a cat does say *"miaow"* and a cow *"moo"* whether they're speaking Spanish or English!

19

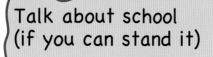

Talk about school
(if you can stand it)

geography
la geografía
👄 la heogra-feeya

PE
la gimnasia
👄 la heem-
naseeya

art
el dibujo artístico
👄 el deebooho
arteesteeko

Spanish
el español
👄 el espanyol

maths
las mates
👄 las mat-tes

20

English
el inglés
🗨 el eeng-les

music
la música
🗨 la mooseeka

science
las naturales
🗨 las natoorar-les

history
la historia
🗨 la eestoreeya

21

IT
TI
 tay-ee

## Way unfair!

Spanish children hardly ever have to wear uniform to school and have very long holidays: 10 weeks in the summer and another 5–6 weeks throughout the rest of the year. But before you turn green with envy, you might not like the mounds of *"deberes para las vacaciones"* (*debair-res para las bakathee-yones*), that's "vacation homework"! And if you fail your exams, the teachers could make you repeat the whole year with your little sister!

# Talk about your phone

That's ancient
¡Qué anticuado!
🗨 kay antee-kwado

I've run
out of credit
Me he quedado
sin saldo
🗨 may ay
kay- dado seen
saldo

What's your mobile
phone like?
¿Cómo es tu móvil?
🗨 komo es too mo-beel

Lucky!
¡Qué suerte!
🗨 kay swair-tay

What a cool ringtone!
¡Qué tono más chulo!
🗨 kay tone-oh mass choolo

# Gossip

**Can you keep a secret?**
¿Puedes guardar
un secreto?
🗣 pwedes
gwardar
oon sekreto

**Do you have a boyfriend (a girlfriend)?**
¿Tienes novio (novia)?
🗣 tee-enes nobyo
(nobya)

**An OK guy/An OK girl**
Un tío majo/
Una tía maja
🗣 oon teeyo maho/
oona teeya maha

**What a bossy-boots!**
¡Qué mandón!
🗣 kay man-don

**He/She's nutty!**
¡Está como una cabra!
🗣 esta komo oona
kabra
*That means "He/She's like a goat"!*

I'm not like
that at all!

**What a misery guts!**
¡Qué malasombra!
🗣 kay malas-sombra

24

## You won't make many friends saying this!

Bog off!
¡Vete a la porra!
*betay a la porra*

Shut up!
¡Cállate!
*kigh-yatay*

If you're fed up with someone, and you want to say something like "you silly ...!" or "you stupid ...!", you can start with *"pedazo de"* (which actually means "piece of ...") and add anything you like. What about ...

Stupid banana!
*¡Pedazo de plátano!*
(*pedatho day platano*)

or ...

Silly sausage!
*¡Pedazo de salchicha!*
(*pedatho day salcheecha*)

Take your pick. It should do the trick. You could also try *"¡pedazo de idiota!"* (*pedatho day eedee-ota*). You don't need a translation here, do you?

# You might have to say

Bother!
¡Ostras!
🗨 os-stras
That means "Oysters"!

Rats!
¡Porras!
🗨 porras

"Did someone call us?"

That's not funny
No tiene gracia
🗨 no tee-enay
gra-theeya

10 tons

That's plenty!
¡Ya vale!
🗨 ya balay

I'm fed up
¡Estoy harto! (boys)
¡Estoy harta! (girls)
🗨 estoy arto/estoy arta

Stop! ¡No hagas eso!

no agas eso

I want to go home!
¡Me quiero ir a casa!

may kyairo eer
ah kassa

I don't care
Me da igual
may da eegwal

At last!
¡Por fin!
por feen

27

# Saying goodbye

Here's my address
Aquí tienes mi dirección
👄 akee tee-enes mee
deerek-thyon

What's your address?
¿Cuál es tu dirección?
👄 kwal es too
deerek-thyon

Come to visit me
Ven a visitarme
 ben a beesee-tarmay

**Have a good trip!**
¡Buen viaje!
 bwen bee-ahay

**Write to me soon**
Escríbeme pronto
 eskree-bemay pronto

**Send me a text**
Envíame un SMS
envee-armay oon "SMS"

**Let's chat online**
¿Chateamos?
chatay-amos

**Bye!**
¡Adiós
adeeyos

**What's your email address?**
¿Cuál es tu mail?
kwal es too mail

*⅃□*@3◇*@𝓝.com

**WANNA PLAY?**

skipping rope
el elástico
el elasteeko

table tennis
el ping-pong
el "ping-pong"

MP3 player
el reproductor
👄 el raypro-dooktor

yo-yo
el yo-yó
👄 el "yo yo"

mobile phone
el móvil
👄 el mo-beel

WANNA PLAY?

Do you want to play ...?
¿Quieres jugar ...?
👄 keyair-res hoogar

... table football?
... al futbolín?
👄 al footboleen

... cards?
... a las cartas?
👄 a las kartas

... on the computer?
... con el ordenador?
👄 kon el orden-ador

... noughts and crosses?
... a las tres en raya?
👄 a las trays en righ-ya

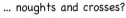

... hide and seek?
... al escondite?
al eskon-deetay

... catch?
... al balón?
al ballon

Not now
Ahora no
a-ora no

Yeah!
¡Vale!
balay

33

## Fancy a game of **foal** or **donkey**?!

In Spain, you don't play "leap frog", you play "foal" – *el potro*. There is also a group version of this called "donkey" – *el burro*. This involves two teams. Team 1 line up in a row with their heads down in the shape of a donkey. Team 2 take it in turns to leap as far as they can onto the back of the "donkey". If the donkey falls over, Team 2 win. If Team 2 touch the ground or can't leap far enough to get all the team on, then Team 1 win – got that?! Spanish children will try to tell you this is enormous fun, but your parents might not be so keen on the bruises!

Can my friend play too?
¿Mi amigo también puede jugar?
👄 mee ameego tam-byen
pway-day hoogar

I have to ask my parents
Se lo tengo que pedir a mis padres
👄 say loe tengo kay pedeer
ah mees padrays

Make yourself heard

Whose turn is it?
¿A quién le toca?
a keeyen lay toka

It's your turn
Te toca a ti
tay toka
a tee

It's my turn
Me toca a mí
may toka
a mee

Can I have a turn?
¿Puedo tirar?
pwedo teer-rar

# Who dares?

You're it!
¡La quedas tú!
🗣 la kedas too

Race you!
¿Una carrera?
🗣 oona karraira

I'm first
Soy el primero (boys)
Soy la primera (girls)
🗣 soy el preemairo
soy la preemaira

Who's winning?

¿Quién gana?

🗣 keeyen gana

Ready, steady, go!

Preparados, listos, ¡ya!

🗣 pray-parados, leestos, yah

Where's the finish?

¿Dónde está la meta?

🗣 donday esta la mayta

I need a head start

Necesito ventaja

🗣 naythay-seeto benta-ha

# Electronic games

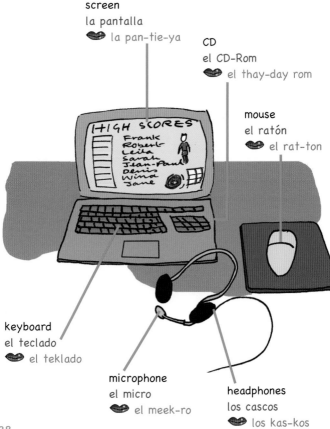

**screen**
la pantalla
👄 la pan-tie-ya

**CD**
el CD-Rom
👄 el thay-day rom

**mouse**
el ratón
👄 el rat-ton

**keyboard**
el teclado
👄 el teklado

**microphone**
el micro
👄 el meek-ro

**headphones**
los cascos
👄 los kas-kos

38

Show me
Enséñame
 ensay-nyamay

What do I do?
¿Qué hay que hacer?
kay eye kay athair

Am I dead?
¿Me han matado?
may an matado

Shoot-em-up!
¡Dispárales!
deespar-ralayz

How many lives do I have?
¿Cuántas vidas tengo?
kwantas beedas tengo

How many levels are there?
¿Cuántos niveles hay?
kwantos neebay-les eye

39

# It's virtual fun!

Do you have WiFi?
¿Tienes wifi?
👄 teeyenes weefee

*Make sure you say it like this to avoid blank looks!*

Send me a message.
Mándame un mensaje.

How do i join?
¿Cómo me apunto?

I'm not old enough.
No tengo edad suficiente.

I'm not allowed.
No tengo permiso.

I don't know who you are.
No te conozco.

my blog
mi blog
👄 mee blog

my friends
mis amigos
👄 mees ameegos

my photos
mis fotos
👄 mees fotos

my videos
mis videos
👄 mees bee-dayos

my music mi música
👄 mee mooseeka

41

# Non couch-potato activities!

tennis
el tenis
🗣 el tenees

trampolining
el trampolín
🗣 el "trampoline"

bowling
los bolos
🗣 los bol-los

swimming
la natación
🗣 la nata-thyon

42

hockey
el hockey
👄 el "hockey"

gymnastics
la gimnasia
👄 la heem-nasya

ballet
el ballet
👄 el ballay

basketball
el baloncesto
👄 el ballon-thesto

and, of course, we haven't forgotten "*el fútbol*"... (P.T.O.)

# football

boots
las botas
🗣 las botas

football kit
el equipo de fútbol
🗣 el ekeepo day footbol

ref
el árbitro
🗣 el arbeetro

shin pads
las espinilleras
🗣 las espinee-yeras

Good save!
¡Vaya parada!
🗣 baya parada

Pass! ¡Pasa!
🗣 pasa

44

Offside!
¡Offside!
💬 just say it!

Hands!
¡Mano!
💬 mano

You're on
my team
Tú estás
en mi equipo
💬 too estas en
mee ekeepo

crossbar
el larguero
💬 el largairo

goalpost
el palo
💬 el pallo

goal
el gol
💬 el gol

goalie
el portero
💬 el portairo

45

defender
el defensa
🗣 el day-fensa

attacker
el delantero
🗣 el daylan-tairo

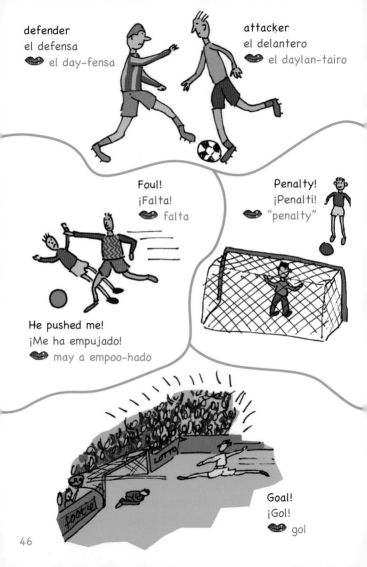

Foul!
¡Falta!
🗣 falta

He pushed me!
¡Me ha empujado!
🗣 may a empoo-hado

Penalty!
¡Penalti!
🗣 "penalty"

Goal!
¡Gol!
🗣 gol

# Keeping the others in line

Not like that!
¡Así no!
 asee no

You cheat! ¡Tramposo! (boys only)
¡Tramposa! (girls only)
 tramposo/tramposa

I'm not playing
anymore
Ya no juego
 ya no hwego

It's not fair!
¡No es justo!
 no es hoosto

Stop it!
¡No hagas eso!
 no agas eso

47

# Showing off

... do a handstand?
... hacer el pino?
 athair el peeno

Can you ...
¿Sabes ...
 sabays

Look at me!
¡Mírame!
meera-may

 ... do a cartwheel?
... dar volteretas
laterales?
dar boltair-
retas latairal-les

... do this?
... hacer esto?
 athair esto

48

Tongue tied

I'd kill for a nice juicy steak!

## Impress your Spanish friends with this!

You can show off to your new Spanish friends by practising this tongue twister:

*Tres tristes tigres comían trigo en un trigal.*
*trays treestays teegrays comee-an treego en oon treegal*
(This means "Three sad tigers ate wheat in a wheat field".)

Then see if they can do as well with this English one:
"She sells seashells on the seashore, but the shells she sells aren't seashells, I'm sure."

# For a rainy day

**pack of cards**
una baraja de cartas
🗣 oona baraha day kartas

**my deal/your deal**
yo doy/tú das
🗣 yo doy/too das

**king**
el rey
🗣 el ray

**queen**
la reina
🗣 la ray-eena

**jack**
la jota
🗣 la hota

**joker**
el komodín
🗣 el komodeen

tréboles
🗣 trebol-les

corazones
🗣 korazon-nes

picas
🗣 peekas

diamantes
🗣 dee-amantays

## Do you have the ace of swords?!

You might also see Spanish children playing with a different pack of cards. There are only 48 cards instead of 52 and the suits are also different. Instead of clubs, spades, diamonds and hearts, there are gold coins (*oros*), swords (*espadas*), cups (*copas*) and batons (*bastos*).

bishop el alfil
el alfeel

chessboard el tablero
el tablairo

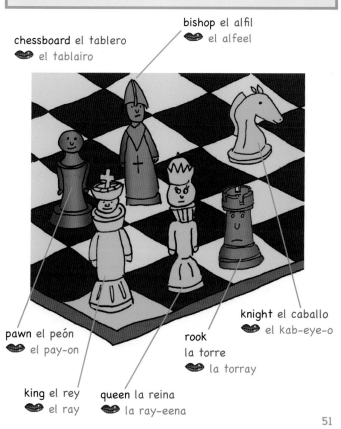

knight el caballo
el kab-eye-o

pawn el peón
el pay-on

rook
la torre
la torray

king el rey
el ray

queen la reina
la ray-eena

51

# FEELING HUNGRY

hamburger
la hamburguesa
👄 la amboorgaysa

chips
las patatas fritas
👄 las patatas freetas

ice cream
el helado
👄 el elardo

Fries

Cola

coke
una coca
👄 oona koka

squid
los calamares
🗣 los kalamar-res

creme caramel
el flan
🗣 el flan
(Watch out! "Flan" in Spanish doesn't mean a pastry tart with cheese!)

paella
la paella
🗣 la pie-eyya

orange juice
el zumo de naranja
🗣 el thoomo day naran-ha

FEELING HUNGRY

# Grub

I'm starving
Tengo un hambre de lobo
 tengo oon ambray day lobo

That means "I have the hunger of a wolf"!

el lobo

Please can I have ...
Por favor, me da ...
 por fabor, may da

... a croissant
un cruasán
 oon krwasan

... a cream bun
un bollo con nata
 oon boyo kon nata

... a puff pastry
una palmera
 oona palmayra

... a waffle
un gofre
oon go-fray

... a muffin
una magdalena
oona magda-layna

55

los churros

 los choorros

These are wonderful sugary doughnut-like snacks. They are sold in cafés and kiosks and usually come in a paper cone. They are also very popular for breakfast in winter, with thick hot chocolate (*chocolate con churros*).

**You:** Can I have some churros, Mum?

**Mum:** No. They'll make you fat and rot your teeth.

**You:** But I think it's good to experience a foreign culturethrough authentic local food.

**Mum:** Oh, all right then.

---

Churros? "*¡Mm, mm!*", Garlic sandwich? "*¡Agh!*". If you're going to make foody noises you'll need to know how to do it properly in Spanish! "Yum, yum!" is out in Spanish. You should say "*¡Mm, mm!*". And "Yuk!" is "*¡Agh!*" (pronounced "*ag*"), but be careful not to let adults hear you say this!

## Drink up

I'm dying for
a drink
Me muero de sed
👄 may mwero
day sed

I'd like ...
Me apetece ...
👄 may
apay-taythay

... a coke
... una coca
👄 oona koka

... an orange juice
... un zumo de naranja
👄 oon thoomo day naran-ha

... an apple juice
... un zumo de manzana
👄 oon thoomo day
manthana

57

... a lemonade
una Fanta® de limón

💋 oona Fanta day leemon

In Spain ask for *una Fanta® de limón* when you want a lemonade or *Fanta® de naranja* (*fanta day naranha*) for a fizzy orange. Fanta® is the most popular type and so that's what people say.

... water agua

💋 agwa

... a milkshake
... un batido

💋 oon bateedo

You get your hot chocolate in a large cup (to dunk your churros in).

... a hot chocolate
... un chocolate

💋 oon chokolatay

# How did you like it?

**That's lovely**
Eso está super bueno
🗣 eso esta soopair bweno

**That's gorgeous**
Eso está delicioso
🗣 eso esta daylee-thee-oso

**I don't like that**
Eso no me gusta
🗣 eso no may goosta

**I'm stuffed**
Voy a explotar
🗣 boy a explotar

**I can't eat that**
No me lo puedo comer
🗣 no may lo pwedo komair

**That's gross**
Está asqueroso
🗣 esta askairoso

## Tap into *Tapas*

There's a perfect way to try a little bit of everything in Spain and that's "*tapas*". These are little snacks that everyone eats in cafés and bars (which the adults might insist on going to). *Tapas* come in little dishes and are a great way of finding out if you like something without risking a torrent of abuse if you leave an expensive meal untouched.

Here are four of the most popular:

tortilla
 tortee-ya
Spanish omelette – thick and comes in slices

croquetas
 kroketas

egg-shaped rissoles filled with chicken, ham or fish

albóndigas
 albon-deegas
meatballs in tomato sauce

calamares a la romana
 kalamar-res a la romana

squid rings

**Parties**

balloon el globo
 el glow-bo

Can I have some more?
¿Puedo tener un poco más?
 pwaydo tenair oon poko mas

party hat
el gorro de fiesta
 el gorro day fee-esta

This is for you
Esto es para ti
 esto es para tee

61

LOOKING GOOD

strap top
el top
🔊 el "top"

bracelets
las pulseras
🔊 las pool-
sairas

shorts
los pantalones
cortos
🔊 los panta-
lone-nes kortos

belt
el cinturón
🔊 el
theen-tooron

leg warmers
los
calientapiernas
🔊 los
kaleeyenta-
peeyairnas

ballet flats
las manoletinas
🔊 las manolay-
teenas

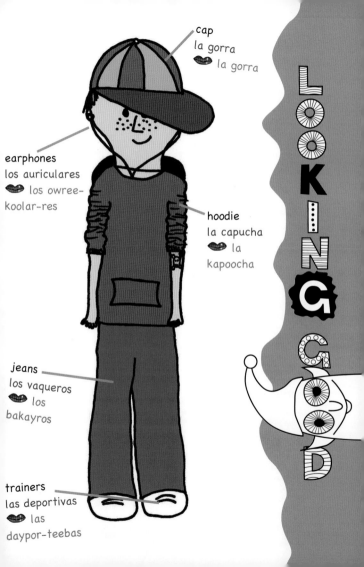

cap
la gorra
🗣 la gorra

earphones
los auriculares
🗣 los owree-
koolar-res

hoodie
la capucha
🗣 la
kapoocha

jeans
los vaqueros
🗣 los
bakayros

trainers
las deportivas
🗣 las
daypor-teebas

LOOKING GOOD

# Clothes

jeans
los vaqueros
los bakayros

sweatshirt
la sudadera
la sooda-dayra

T-shirt
la camiseta
la kameeseta

football shirt
la camiseta de fútbol
la kameeseta day footbol

trainers
las deportivas
las daypor-teebas

shoes
los zapatos
los thapatos

skirt
la falda
🗣 la falda

dress
el traje
🗣 el trahay

trousers
los pantalones
🗣 los panta-lone-nes

## A pair of cowboys?

The word for jeans in Spanish (*los vaqueros* – *los bakayros*) actually means "cowboys" because they were the first people to wear these trousers.

That T-shirt, please
Esa camiseta, por favor
🗨 esa kameeseta, por fabor

Cool tattoo!
¡Qué calcamonía más chula!
🗨 kay kalka-moneeya mass choola

The pink frilly one
La rosa con volantitos
🗨 la rosa kon bolanteetos

Awesome miniskirt!
¡Vaya minifalda mas chula!
🗨 baya meenee falda mass choola

The purple stripey one
La morada de rayas
🗨 la morada day right-yas

spotty
de lunares
🗣 day loonar-res

flowery
de flores
🗣 day flor-res

frilly
con volantitos
🗣 kon bolanteetos

glittery
con brillos
🗣 kon breeyos

stripey
de rayas
🗣 day righ-yas

67

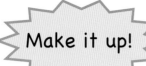

# Make it up!

lip gloss
el Brillo de labios
🖤 el breeyo
day labyos

nail varnish
el pintauñas
🖤 el peentaw-nyas

glitter gel
la brillantina
🖤 la breeyan-teena

earrings
los pendientes
🖤 los pend-yentays

I need a mirror
Necesito un espejo
🖤 netthayseeto
oon espay-ho

eye shadow
la sombra de ojos
🖤 la sombray day
o-hos

Can I borrow your
straighteners?
¿Me dejas tu
alisador de pelo?
🖤 may day-has too
alee-sadoor day pay-lo

colours
los colores
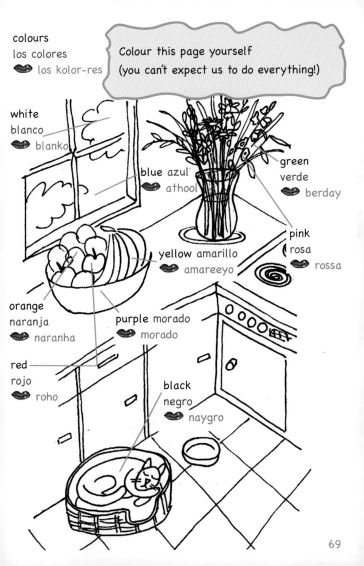 los kolor-res

Colour this page yourself
(you can't expect us to do everything!)

white
blanco
blanko

blue azul
athool

green
verde
berday

pink
rosa
rossa

yellow amarillo
amareeyo

orange
naranja
naranha

purple morado
morado

red
rojo
roho

black
negro
naygro

69

What should we do?
¿Qué hacemos?
🗣 kay athay-mos

Can I come?
¿Puedo ir?
🗣 pwedo eer

Where do you all hang out?
¿Por dónde salís vosotros?
🗣 por donday salees bos-otros

That's really wicked
Eso es chachi
🗣 eso es chachee

I'm (not) allowed
(No) me dejan
🗣 (no) may day-han

72

Let's go back Regresemos
 regray-saymos

That gives me
goose bumps
(or "chicken flesh"
in Spanish!)
Eso me pone la
carne de gallina
 eso may ponay la
karnay day gayeena

I'm bored to death
Me muero de aburrimiento
 may mwero day
aburree-mee-ento

HOUSE OF
MIRRORS

That's a laugh
Te ríes cantidad
 tay reeyes kanteedad

# Beach babes

Can I borrow this?
¿Me dejas esto?
👄 may dehas esto

Let's hit the beach
Vamos a la playa
👄 bamos a la playa

Is this your bucket?
¿Es tuyo este cubo?
👄 es tooyo estay koobo

You can bury me
Me puedes enterrar
👄 pay pwedes entair-rar

Stop throwing sand!
¡Deja de echar arena!
👄 dayha day echar arayna

Mind my eyes!
¡Cuidado con mis ojos!
👄 kweedado kon mees ohos

**sandcastle**
el castillo de arena
🗣 el casteeyo
day arayna

**sea**
el mar
🗣 el mar

**beach** la playa
🗣 la playa

**towel**
la toalla
🗣 la toe-aya

**swimming costume**
el bañador
🗣 el banyador

**bucket** el cubo
🗣 el koobo

**snorkel**
el tubo
🗣 el toobo

**shells**
las conchas
🗣 las konchas

**spade**
la pala
🗣 la palla

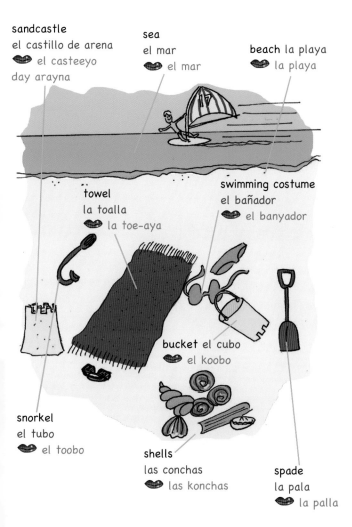

# It's going swimmingly!

*How to make a splash in Spanish!*

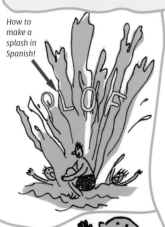

PLOF

Let's hit the swimming pool
Vamos a la piscina
 bamos a la peeseena

Can you swim (underwater)?
¿Sabes nadar (debajo del agua)? sabays nadar (debaho del agwa)

Me too/I can't
Yo también/Yo no
yo tambeeyen/yo no

Can you dive?
¿Te sabes tirar de cabeza?
tay sabays teerar day kabaytha

I'm getting changed
Me estoy cambiando
may estoy kambee-ando

Can you swim ...?
¿Sabes nadar ...?
👄 sabays nadar

... backstroke
a espalda
👄 a espalda

... butterfly
a mariposa
👄 a mareeposa

... crawl
a crol
👄 a krol

... breaststroke
a braza 👄 a bratha

slide
el tobogán
👄 el tobogan

goggles
las gafas
👄 las gafas

77

# Downtown

Do you know the way?
¿Te sabes el camino?
🗣 tay sabays el kameeno

## Pooper-scoopers on wheels!

You might see bright green-and-white motorcycles with funny vacuum cleaners on the side riding around town scooping up the dog poop. The people riding the bikes look like astronauts! (Well, you'd want protection too, wouldn't you?)

Let's ask
Vamos a preguntar
🗣 bamos a pray-goontar

bus
el autobús
🗣 el owtoboos

78

**Is it far?**
¿Está lejos?
🗨 esta lay-hos

**Are we allowed in here?**
¿Nos dejan entrar aquí?
🗨 nos day-han entrar akee

**car**
el coche
🗨 el kochay

You could gain a lot of street cred with your new Spanish friends by using a bit of slang. A clapped-out car is *"una cafetera"* (*oona cafaytayra*), which means "coffee pot"! Try this: *"¡Vaya cafetera!"* (*baya cafaytayra* – "What an old banger!").

# Park yourself here

swings **los columpios**
🗣 los koloom-peeyos

climbing frame **el juego para escalar** 🗣 el hway-go para eska-lar

playground **el patio de recreo**
🗣 el pateeyo day rekrayo

grass **la hierba**
🗣 la yairba

tree **el árbol**
🗣 el ar-bol

slide
**el tobogán**
🗣 el tobogan

park **el parque** 🗣 el parkay

80

Can we play ball games?
¿Podemos jugar a la pelota?
🗨 poday-mos hoo-gar a la pay-lota

roundabout
el tiovivo
🗨 el tio-beebo

sandpit
el arenero
🗨 el arain-airo

Can I have a go? ¿Puedo intentarlo?
🗨 pwaydo intain-tarloe

# Picnics

I hate wasps
Odio las avispas
👄 odeeyo las
abeespas

Move over!
¡Apártate!
👄 apar-tatay

bread
el pan 👄 el pan

Shall we sit here?
¿Nos sentamos aquí?
👄 nos sentamos
akee

napkin
la servilleta
👄 la serbeeyeta

ham el jamón
👄 el hamon

cheese
el queso
👄 el kayso

yoghurt
el yogurt
👄 el yogurt

crisps
las patatas fritas
👄 las patatas
freetas

82

**drinks**
**las bebidas**
🗣 las bebeedas

**knife**
**el cuchillo**
🗣 el koocheeyo

**spoon**
**la cuchara**
🗣 la koochara

**fork**
**el tenedor**
🗣 el tenaydor

**bees**
**las abejas**
🗣 las abayhas

**wasps**
**las avispas**
🗣 las abeespas

bzzzz

**ants**
**las hormigas**
🗣 las ormeegas

# Wake up, campers!

tent la tienda
🗨 la tyen-da

tent peg la piqueta
🗨 la pee-kayta

camper van
la caravana
🗨 la kara-vana

penknife
la navaja de bolsillo
🗨 la nava-ha day
bol-seelyo

camping stove
el camping gas
🗨 el "camping gas"

sleeping bag el saco de dormir
🗨 el sak-ko day door-meer

torch la linterna
🗨 la lintair-na

84

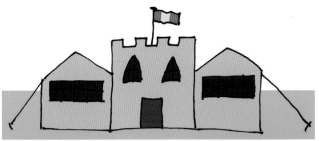

That tent's a palace!
Jo, ¡vaya tienda!
ho, buy-ya tyen-da

Is there a campfire?
¿Hay una hoguera?
ay oona og-waira

I've lost my torch
He perdido mi linterna
eh pairdeedo mee lintair-na

These showers are gross!
¡Las duchas están sucias!
las doo-chas estan soothyas

Where does the rubbish go?
¿Dónde se tira la basura?
donday say teera la basoora

# All the fun of the fair

big wheel
la noria
👄 la noreeya

helter-skelter
el tobogán
👄 el tobogan

house of mirrors
la casa de los espejos
👄 la kasa day los espayhos

Shall we go on this?
¿Nos montamos en éste?
👄 nos montamos en estay

bumper cars
los coches de choque
👄 los kochays day chokay

86

roundabout
el pulpo
 el poolpo

It's very fast
Va muy rápido
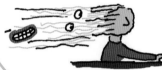 ba mwee rapeedo

That's for babies
Eso es para los pequeños
eso es para los
pekay-nyos

Do you get wet in here?
¿En éste te mojas?
 en estay tay mohas

I'm not going on my own
Yo solo no me monto
 yo solo no may monto

# Disco nights

mirror ball
la bola de espejos
🗣 la bola day espay-hos

loudspeaker
el altavoz
🗣 el altab-oth

Can I request a song?
¿Puedo pedir una canción?
🗣 pwaydo paydeer oona kan-thyon

The music is really lame
¡La música es malísima!
🗣 la mooseeka es malee-seema

DJ
el pinchadiscos
🗣 el peencha-deeskos

spotlights
los focos
🗣 los fo-kos

turntable
el tocadiscos
🗣 el toka-deeskos

How old do I
need to be?
¿Cuántos años
hay que tener?
🗨 kwantos anyos
ay kay tenair

dance floor
la pista de baile
🗨 la peesta day balay

Let's dance!
¡Vamos a bailar!
🗨 ba-mos a balar

I love this song!
¡Me encanta
esta canción!
🗨 may enkanta
esta kan-thyon

# POCKET MONEY

sweets
los caramelos
👄 los karamaylos

T-shirts
las camisetas
👄 las kameesetas

toys
los juguetes
👄 los hoogetes

shop assistant
el tendero
👄 el tendayro

**books**
los libros
 los leebros

**pencils**
los lápices
 los lapeethes

**POCKET MONEY**

# What does that sign say?

butcher shop
carnicería
🗣 karneethereeya

cake shop
pastelería
🗣 pasteler
-reeya

bakery
panadería
🗣 panadereeya

sweet shop
confitería
🗣 confeeter-
reeya

greengrocer
verdulería
🗣 berdooler-
reeya

stationers
papelería
🗣 papelereeya

clothes shop
boutique
🗣 booteek

Do you have some cash?
¿Tienes pasta?
💬 tee-enes pasta

I'm broke
No tengo un duro
💬 no tengo oon dooro

I'm loaded
Estoy forrado
💬 estoy forrado

Here you go
Aquí tienes
💬 akee tee-enes

That's a weird shop!
¡Vaya tienda más rara!
💬 buy-ya tyen-da mas ra-ra

That's a bargain Eso es una ganga 💬 eso es oona ganga

It's a rip-off
Es un robo
💬 es oon robo

# Sweet heaven!

**I love this shop**
Me encanta esta tienda
👄 may enkanta esta
tee-enda

**Let's get some sweets**
Vamos a comprar chucherías
👄 bamos a comprar
choochereeyas

**Let's get some ice cream**
Vamos por un helado
👄 bamos por oon aylado

**lollipops**
las piruletas
👄 las peerooletas

**a bar of chocolate**
una tableta de chocolate
👄 oona tableta day
chokolatay

**chewing gum**
el chicle
👄 el cheeklay

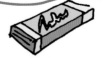

If you really want to look Italian and end up with lots of fillings, ask for:

### regaliz

(regaleez)

*soft licorice sticks, available in red or black*

### polvos pica-pica
(polvos peeka peeka)

*tangy fizzy sherbet sold in small packets with a lollipop to dip in*

### Chupa-chups®
(choopa-choops)

*lollies famous all over the world, but they come from Spain*

### jamones

(hamon-nes)

*fruity, fizzy gums in the shape of hams ("ham" is jamón)*

### nubes (noobes)
*soft marshmallow sweets ("flumps") in different shades (nubes means clouds)*

### kilométrico

(keelomay-treeko)

*chewing gum in a strip like dental floss – pretend to the adults that you're flossing your teeth!*

# Other things you could buy

(that won't ruin your teeth!)

**What are you getting?**
¿Qué te vas a comprar?
🫦 kay tay bas a komprar

**That toy, please**
Ese juguete, por favor
🫦 esay hoogetay, por fabor

**Two postcards, please**
Dos postales, por favor
🫦 dos postal-les, por fabor

**This is rubbish**
Esto es una porquería
🫦 esto es oona porkayreeya

**This is cool**
Esto mola
🫦 esto mola

I'm getting ...
Voy a comprar
 boy a comprar

... a pen
... un boli
 oon bolee

... stamps
... sellos
 seyos

... felt-tip pens
... rotuladores
 rotooladior-res

... coloured pencils
... lápices de colores
 lapeethes day kolor-res

... a key ring
... un llavero
 oon yabairo

... comics
... tebeos
 taybayos

... a shell box
... un joyero de conchas
👄 oon ho-yairo day konchas

... a fridge magnet
... un imán de nevera
👄 oon ee-man day nay-baira

... a necklace
un collar
👄 oon koyar

How much is that?
¿Cuánto cuesta?
👄 kwanto kwesta

For many years Spain's favourite comics have been *Mortadelo y Filemón*, two accident-prone TIA agents (not CIA) and *Zipi y Zape*, two very naughty twins. Children also like to read *Mafalda*, an Argentinian comic, *Carlitos y Snoopy* (Charlie Brown & Snoopy), Tintin, Astérix and *¿Dónde está Wally?* (Where's Wally?).

# Money talks

How much pocket
money do you get?
¿Cuánto te dan de paga?
🫦 kwanto tay dan day pa-ga

I only have this much
Sólo tengo esto
🫦 soul-lo tain-go esto

Can you lend me
ten euros?
¿Me prestas
diez euros?
🫦 may praystas
deeyeth ay-ooros

No way!
¡Ni hablar!
🫦 nee ablar

Spanish money is the euro (pronounced *ay-ooro*).
A euro is divided into 100 centimos (*thainteemos*).
Coins:    1, 2, 5, 10, 20, 50 centimos
              1, 2 euros
Notes:    5, 10, 20, 50, 100 euros
Make sure you know how much you are spending before you
blow all your pocket money at once!

# GROWN UP TALK

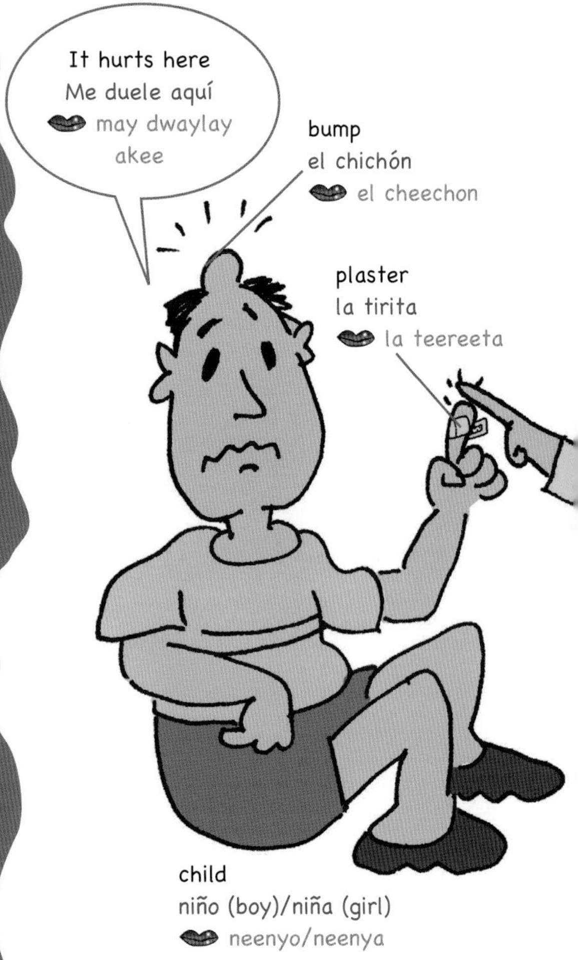

Help!

Something has dropped/broken
Algo se ha caído/roto
👄 algo say a kigh-eedo/roto

Please
Por favor
👄 por fabor

Can you help me?
¿Me puedes ayudar?
👄 may pwedes ayoodar

Where's the post box?
¿Dónde está el buzón?
👄 donday esta el boothon

Where are the toilets?
¿Dónde están los aseos?
👄 donday estan los asayos

I can't manage it
No puedo
 no pwedo

Could you pass me that?
¿Me pasas eso?
 may pasas eso

What time is it?
¿Qué hora es?
kay ora es

Come and see
Ven a ver
 ben a bair

May I look at your watch?
¿Me deja que mire su reloj?
may deha kay meera
soo reloh

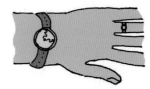

# Lost for words

I've lost ...
He perdido ...
👄 eh perdeedo

... my ticket
mi billete
👄 mee beeyaytay

... my parents
mis padres
👄 mees padrays

... my mobile
mi móvil
👄 mee mo-beel

... my money mi dinero
mee deenayro

... my shoes
mis zapatos
mees thapatos

... my jumper
mi jersey
mee hersay

... my watch
mi reloj
mee reloh

... my jacket mi chaqueta
mee chakayta

# Adults only!

Show this page to adults who can't seem to make themselves clear (it happens). They will point to a phrase, you read what they mean, and you should all understand each other perfectly.

No te preocupes
Don't worry

Siéntate aquí
Sit down here

¿Tu nombre y apellidos?
What's your name and surname?

¿Cuántos años tienes?
How old are you?

¿De dónde eres?
Where are you from?

¿Dónde te alojas?
Where are you staying?

¿Dónde te duele?
Where does it hurt?

¿Eres alérgico a algo?
Are you allergic to anything?

Está prohibido
It's forbidden

Tiene que acompañarte un adulto
You have to have an adult with you

Voy por alguien que hable inglés
I'll get someone who speaks English

**EXTRA STUFF**

weather
el tiempo
 el tyem-po

numbers los números  los noo-mairos

time
la hora
🫦 la ora

EXTRA STUFF

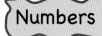

## Numbers

Knock, knock.

Who's there?

Uno.

Uno who?

Unos where I got this crummy joke!

1 uno 💋 oono

2 dos 💋 dos

3 tres 💋 trays

4 cuatro 💋 kwatro

5 cinco 💋 theenko

6 seis 💋 sayis

**7 siete**
🗣 see-etay

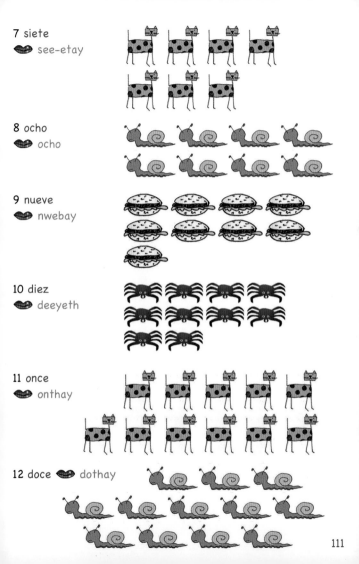

**8 ocho**
🗣 ocho

**9 nueve**
🗣 nwebay

**10 diez**
🗣 deeyeth

**11 once**
🗣 onthay

**12 doce** 🗣 dothay

**13** trece  trethay

**14** catorce  katorthay

**15** quince  keenthay

112

| 16 | dieciséis | *deeyethee sayis* |
| 17 | diecisiete | *deeyethee see-etay* |
| 18 | dieciocho | *deeyethee ocho* |
| 19 | diecinueve | *deeyethee nwebay* |

> If you want to say "thirty-two", "fifty-four" and so on, you can just put the two numbers together like you do in English. But don't forget to add the word for "and" (*y* – *ee*) in the middle:
>
> | 32 | treinta y dos | *traynta ee dos* |
> | 54 | cincuenta y cuatro | *theenkwenta ee kwatro* |
> | 81 | ochenta y uno | *ochenta ee oono* |

| 20 | viente | *baintay* |
| 30 | treinta | *traynta* |
| 40 | cuarenta | *kwarenta* |
| 50 | cincuenta | *theenkwenta* |
| 60 | sesenta | *saysenta* |
| 70 | setenta | *saytenta* |
| 80 | ochenta | *ochenta* |
| 90 | noventa | *nobenta* |
| 100 | cien | *theeyen* |

113

a thousand mil *meel*

a million un millón *oon meel-yon*

a gazillion! tropecientos! *tropay- theeyentos*

| | | |
|---|---|---|
| 1st | primero | *preemairo* |
| 2nd | segundo | *segoondo* |
| 3rd | tercero | *terthayro* |
| 4th | cuarto | *kwarto* |
| 5th | quinto | *keento* |
| 6th | sexto | *sexto* |
| 7th | séptimo | *septeemo* |
| 8th | octavo | *octabo* |
| 9th | noveno | *nobayno* |
| 10th | décimo | *daytheemo* |

## Fancy a date?

If you want to say a date in Spanish, you don't need to use 1st, 2nd, etc. Just say the ordinary number followed by *de* (*day*):

| Lunes | Martes | Miércoles | Jueves | Viernes | Sábado | Domingo |
|---|---|---|---|---|---|---|
| | | 1 | 2 | 3 | 4 | 5 |
| 6 | 7 | 8 | 9 | 10 | 11 | 12 |
| 13 | 14 | 15 | 16 | 17 | 18 | 19 |
| 20 | 21 | 22 | 23 | 24 | 25 | 26 |
| 27 | 28 | 29 | 30 | | | |

uno de marzo
(1st of March)

diez de julio       (10th of July)

# Months

| | | |
|---|---|---|
| March | marzo | *martho* |
| April | abril | *abreel* |
| May | mayo | *my-yo* |

| | | |
|---|---|---|
| June | junio | *hooneeyo* |
| July | julio | *hooleeyo* |
| August | agosto | *agosto* |

| September | septiembre | *septee-embray* |
| October | octubre | *octoobray* |
| November | noviembre | *nobee-embray* |

| December | diciembre | *deethee-embray* |
| January | enero | *enayro* |
| February | febrero | *febrayro* |

## Seasons

primavera    *preemabayra*

SPRING

verano    *berano*

SUMMER

otoño    *otonyo*

AUTUMN

invierno    *eenbee-erno*

WINTER

# Days of the week

| Monday | lunes | *loon-nes* |
|---|---|---|
| Tuesday | martes | *mar-tes* |
| Wednesday | miércoles | *mee-erkol-les* |
| Thursday | jueves | *hoo-ebes* |
| Friday | viernes | *bee-er-nes* |
| Saturday | sábado | *sabado* |
| Sunday | domingo | *domeengo* |

By the way, Spanish kids have a two-and-a-half hour lunch break! Time enough for lunch and a siesta. But they don't finish until 5pm in the afternoon.

# Good times

It's ...
Son ...
👄 sonn

(five) o'clock
las (cinco)
👄 las (theenko)

quarter past (two)
las (dos) y cuarto
👄 las (dos) ee kwarto

quarter to (four)
las (cuatro) menos cuarto
👄 las (kwatro) menos kwarto

half past (three)
las (tres) y media
👄 las (trays) ee medya

**five past (ten)**
las (diez) y cinco
🗣 las (deeyeth)
ee theenko

**twenty past (eleven)**
las (once) y viente
🗣 las (onthay)
ee baintay

**ten to (four)**
las (cuatro) menos diez
🗣 las (kwatro)
menos deeyeth

**twenty to (six)**
las (seis) menos veinte
🗣 las (sayis)
menos baintay

---

Watch out for "one o'clock". It's a bit different from the other times. If you want to say "It's one o'clock" you have to say *Es la una* (*es la oona*). "It's half past one" is *Es la una y media* (*es la oona ee medya*), and so on.

### morning
### mañana
 la manyarna

### midday
### mediodía
la medyo-deeya

### afternoon
### la tarde
la tarday

### evening la noche
la nochay

### midnight
### la medianoche
la medya-nochay

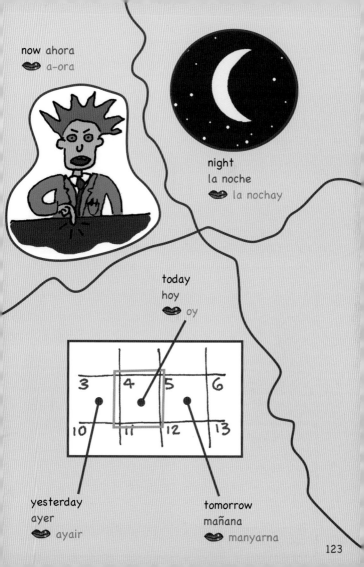

now ahora
a-ora

night
la noche
la nochay

today
hoy
oy

3    4    5    6

10    11    12    13

yesterday
ayer
ayair

tomorrow
mañana
manyarna

123

## Weather wise

It's hot
Hace calor
 athay kalor

Can we go out?
¿Podemos salir fuera?
🗣 podaymos
saleer fwera

It's cold
Hace frío
🗣 athay freeyo

It's horrible
Hace un día horrible
🗣 athay oon deeya
orreeblay

### It's raining seas!

In Spanish it doesn't rain "cats and dogs", it rains "seas"! That's what they say when it's raining really heavily:
*¡Está lloviendo a mares!*
*esta yobeeyendo a mar-res*

**It's windy**
Hace viento
 athay beeyento

**It's sunny**
Hace sol
athay sol

**It's raining**
Está lloviendo
 esta
yobeeyendo

**It's snowing**
Está nevando
 esta nebando

**I'm soaked**
Estoy empapado
 estoy empapardo

**It's nice** Hace bueno
 athay bweno

# Signs of life

altura mínima
minimum Height

Móviles prohibidos
No mobiles

Entrada prohibida
No entry

Sólo mayores
de 18
Over 18s only

Sólo menores de 5
Under 5s only

NO FUNCIONA

OUT OF ORDER

PRIVATE

Privado

Caballeros

Señoras